Success By 3rd Grade
How parents can make
THE DIFFERENCE

3D Learner

Written by Mira and Mark Halpert

This book is dedicated to the families we have worked with, and those that we will in the future. To the children who were struggling, and those that still are. To our professional partners who are critical to helping our children succeed. Our work is dedicated to transforming your academic stress into academic success!

We would like to extend a special thanks to our right-hand colleague Eva Schmeichler. She helped create the necessary tools to help you become a parent **Who Can Make The Difference.**

How You As
Informed, Empowered and Proactive Parents Can Make The Difference

If you knew a Category 5 Hurricane was going to hit your house next summer, and you knew the date and the time, what would you do differently?

Our guess is you would do a number of things differently.

While we cannot forecast hurricanes with that type of accuracy, we know that the 3rd grade reading test that was taken by Florida students in 2015 was the hardest test ever given to Florida 3rd graders. **Three key points to consider**:

1. The text and the questions were both far harder than previous tests.
2. Passing rates are likely to drop far lower than most people expect
3. Third grade retention rates will spike in 2016 when the new cut scores are set, and 1st and 2nd grade retention will increase in 2015/16.

We have been immersed in this issue for several years. Based on our experience, we project that:

A. The percentage of 3rd graders scoring below grade level will increase from 43% to 65% -70%

B. The percentage of 3rd graders who may be subject to 3rd grade retention in 2016 is likely to increase from 19% to 25% to 30 %. This means that 50,000 to 60,000 students face the risk 3rd grade retention in 2016 and beyond.

It gets worse

- A number of 3rd graders promoted to 4th grade in 2015 may be far behind in reading.
- Stress will increase dramatically for 1st and 2nd graders and early grade retention will increase.
- These students will find all subjects much more difficult; reading comprehension will be far more important than ever as it is woven into math, social studies, science assignments, and tests

Who Will This Impact?

This will impact some gifted children, many smart struggling students, virtually all students with dyslexia or a learning disability, and every child with a developmental delay who still takes the test. The new standards are being adopted by all public and charter schools and many private schools.

Negative Impact of These Changes
The present attack on Common Core and the new Florida State Standards is shifting the focus from a key issue – reading comprehension. The average student will be at least one grade level further behind where he or she was previously performing with the older and easier standards. This will be a direct result of reading comprehension being neglected in the past, and a shift to reading comprehension being the foundation of all subjects.

Getting help from public schools has become much harder

Public and charter schools are now using Response to Intervention (RTI) to help students succeed, before assessing the students for special education. This is a 4 step process where:
- Tier I is when a regular teacher tries different strategies. If this gets your child back to grade level, the process may stop; if not, your child moves onto …

- Tier II is where another teacher usually comes into the classroom and will try different strategies. If this gets your child back to grade level the process may stop; if not, your child moves onto …
- Tier III is where your child is often pulled out into a small group setting with another teacher who tries another set of different strategies. If this gets your child back to grade level the process may stop; if not, your child should then be referred to …
- A child study team to consider an evaluation for Special Education Services

In November 2011, Melody Musgrove, the Director of the US Department of Special Education Services, issued a letter saying that RTI cannot be used to delay or deny an evaluation. School personnel should know this, but they may not.

What is worse is that many more children will struggle with reading comprehension and the new Common Core Tests, whether they are in General Education, RTI or Special Education.

While this process sounds good, in reality, many of the struggling students are never identified, and therefore, are neither in RTI nor in Special Education Services. These students often continue to struggle.

3D Learner
Since 1997, 3D Learner, our educational organization, has been helping students to Succeed by 3rd Grade, to pass the Third Grade Reading FCAT, and far more important than that, to have the lifelong skills he or she needs to succeed in school and in life.

Reading Plus, a web-based reading program, has assessed over 44,000 3rd graders nationwide this year, many of whom were not in special education. Based on passages and questions consistent with the new standards, 75% of 3rd graders tested for reading comprehension were 2 to 2.5 years below grade level.

Many Students Will Not Get the Help They Specifically Need from Schools

We come at this from a very different perspective than most. We understand that more than 60% of the students learn differently; we call these students right-brain learners. Like two of our four kids, these right-brain learners learn differently and are far more likely to have problems with visual and auditory processing, attention, anxiety, understanding the meaning of high frequency words (what, but, if, and etc.), and recognizing words the student has previously seen and not mastered.

If this describes your child, the risks are far greater than for a child who learns the way the schools teach.

This book is primarily written for parents and grandparents and is focused on helping you be an Informed, Empowered and Proactive Parent and Grandparent. We include grandparents in the mix, because grandparents frequently recognize that their grandchild learns differently.

Rather than write a long book with a lot of details, we have chosen to write a short book that outlines:

- The **Information** that is most critical to know.

- **Empowerment** strategies to help your child be all he or she can be. We believe parents need to collaborate with schools, find the right programs for their child and integrate the processes. We will share concepts to do all three. We also believe parents need to be empowered to challenge the status quo. When others tell you to be more realistic, but you believe your child has the potential to do far better, you need to be empowered to help your child reach that goal.

- **Proactive Parenting**. We have been rightfully accused of being strong advocates for our own children and others. We firmly believe in collaboration with the schools, as long as the focus is on Success. We have seen proactive parents help their child succeed much earlier than most, and avoid the incredible stress from the 3rd Grade Tests and the consequences.

At the end of this book, we will provide you with access to our no cost on-line assessment, to join us for a group discussion, and a no cost consult on how you can make the difference for your child by the end of the summer or early fall.

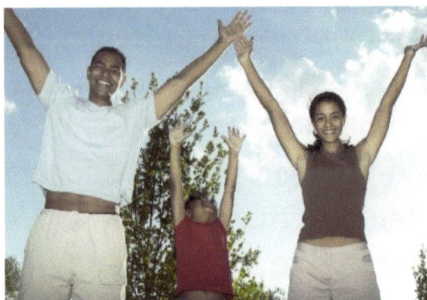

Informed Parents – The Critical Information You Want to Know

The Common Core Standards were initiated by the National Governors Association, and have been strongly supported by the Federal Government, the Gates Foundation, and others. The Common Core Assessments, or ones like them, are the tests being used to test our children in 45 states. When New York became the first state to test all their students with the new Common Core Assessments, the passing rate dropped from 55% to 31% and from 16% to 6% for students with disabilities.

In Florida, there is a 3rd Grade Retention Law that requires 3rd graders who are well below grade level to be retained, unless the student meets other rigorous requirements. While the Florida Legislature has given schools and teachers a one year grace-period before they will feel the negative consequences from the new tests, at present, **your child and others will feel the full force of the 3rd Grade Retention Policy starting in 2014- 2015**.

5 Factors That Impact Reading and Reading Comprehension

We agree with the experts that there are at least 5 key skills needed to become an effective reader. These are phonics, phonemic awareness, fluency, vocabulary, and reading comprehension.

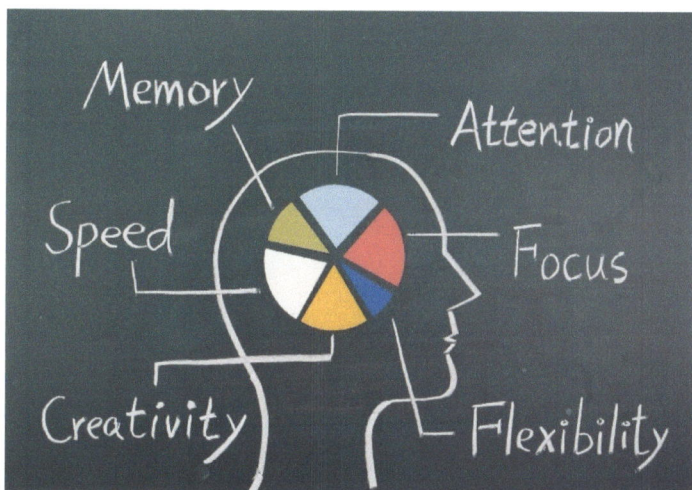

My name is Mira Halpert. I have my Master's degree in Education from the University of Michigan and since 1997, the 3D Learner Program ® I developed has helped thousands of students to improve their reading comprehension, test scores, and so much more. What I have come to realize is that if your child learns differently, there are far more skills that could and often do hold them back.

Below are just seven of them:

- **Visual and auditory processing**
- **Attention**
- **Anxiety and frustration**
- **Knowing what the high frequency words mean**
- **Being able to recognize words your child has seen and not mastered**
- **The ability to understand complex text and questions, that are often meant to trick your child**
- **The ability to be calm and resilient, when faced with a very challenging high stakes test**

Right-brain learners often have several of these factors, and these factors are often not identified or addressed by schools, tutors, or traditional programs.

Visual and auditory processing can interfere with how a child perceives and hears information. These skills are different than visual acuity (how clearly one sees), and hearing. Often these students' hearing abilities are quite keen, especially when conversations are about them. The difficulty comes in the ability to follow complex verbal directions or integrating what they see with what they hear.

Lack of attention is often suggested as the reason a child is not progressing in school. "If only he would pay attention or focus, he could do better", is a recurring response we hear parents report teachers say. When a right-brained learner is engaged and understands what is being presented, attention is not the issue. Students need to learn what being attentive means, and they need to know how to be able to self-regulate.

If a student is struggling, doesn't understand and can't focus, the end result is frustration. We are talking about children who are 6-8 years old having major anxiety attacks because they are not successful readers. I find this unacceptable. These children need to be encouraged and recognized for the abilities they have, and their incredible sensitivities. Yes, these students are extremely emotional. They have wonderful abilities relating to young children, animals, senior citizens, and what they perceive as being unfair.

While research has shown that the phonetic approach to reading is important, most right-brained learners or visual-spatial learners fall through the cracks. These students may be able to learn "the sound of all the letters" but they have a very difficult time sequencing a blending of these sounds to form words. This process is often too slow and tedious for the way they think. They form rapid assumptions, which is a picture of that word. They learn faster from a reading process that "incorporates the use of recognizing and comparing whole words".

As suggested by Betty Maxwell, M.A., associate director of the Gifted Development Center in Denver, CO., "a better way for these children is a personally meaningful whole-word approach. These students do better learning a large number of sight words before approaching phonics analytically."

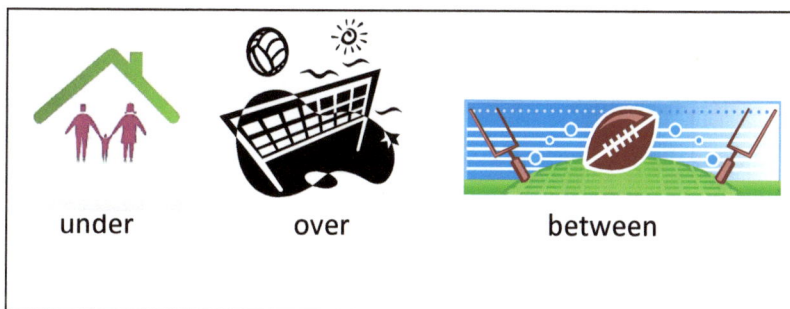

under   over   between

It is important that these students build a large visual vocabulary bank of words they want to learn. It is also vital that they improve their visual memory through playing games to remember the words they have seen. Building visual memory is essential for them in order to be successful readers.

Traditional dyslexia programs, learning center programs, and tutors often focus on a combination of the 5 elements for reading. If your child learns differently or has a combination of issues such as: visual and auditory processing, attention, anxiety, high frequency vocabulary, pattern recognition, understanding complex passages and questions, calming and resilience challenges, **you want to consider a program that identifies and addresses the relevant challenges.**

I learn differently and am a right-brain learner. The results of students we worked with start to tell the picture, but the three key things I want you to understand are:

- A learning difference is often hereditary, although it could be caused by factors like multiple ear infections. Your child's challenges are not the result of something you did or did not do.
- Each of these items is relatively easy to screen for, and a formal assessment can be completed at a reasonable cost.
- If this describes your child, significant results can often be seen in months rather than years. It is very important to recognize that for students with very significant or developmental disabilities, the results are often not the same. Progress can be made, but not at the same rate or magnitude.

Some examples of the students we have helped:

- Every gifted child did extremely well on standardized tests, and a lot of them scored above grade level
- Most smart struggling students also scored above grade level
- Virtually every child with dyslexia or a learning disability passed the test

Their friends often continued to struggle, many were retained, and others spent years in remedial reading. They were not challenged, their chances of being bored sky rocketed, and there were many more students with behavior challenges in their classes.

You may be told that your child will outgrow his or her reading problem. Research shows this is not true (Report on Learning Disabilities Research By: G. Reid Lyon (1997).

- o Almost 90% of the students with a word identification problem in 1st grade will be poor readers in 4th grade
- o Over 70% of the students with a reading disability (dyslexia) in 3rd grade will still have a reading disability (dyslexia) in 12th grade

With the new and much more difficult tests, the future statistics are likely to be even worse.

The last and most important part of the equation is that there are things you can do to make the difference for your child. We have helped students who were going into 2nd or 3rd grade, or were facing 3rd grade retention, make dramatic gains. Below are just three examples:

- A 2nd grader had a zero Lexile score. Her comprehension was really low. 6 weeks later she was close to grade level, and on the 3rd Grade FCAT she was above grade level.

- A 3rd grader's parents were told at the beginning of the school year that she would not pass the 3rd grade FCAT, and that she would almost certainly be subject to 3rd grade retention. She actually scored above grade level on the test.

- A 3rd grader failed the 3rd grade FCAT and later scored at the 74th percentile on the End of Summer Test. (This is one of the qualifying items that allow a student to be promoted to 4th grade.)

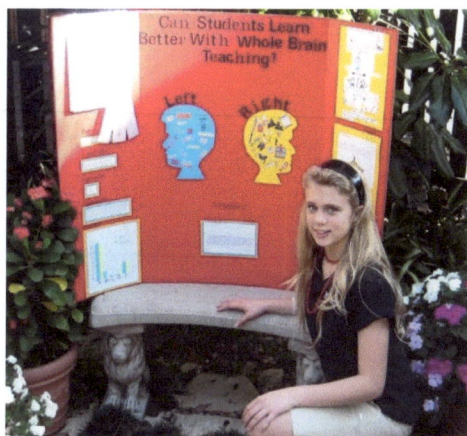

Empowered Parents Make the Difference

We have been very fortunate to work with some of the best and most committed parents. Skeptics have correctly told us that we have a real advantage because we work with dedicated parents. We believe that is true, and that is our focus.

As a parent, you are in a situation where your child is facing a very, very difficult school and testing situation. Some have chosen to protest, others to leave for a private school, and others to home school their child. We strongly encourage you to be empowered to help your child be successful in whatever school setting you choose. Just be sure your child receives all the support needed to make that happen.

In addition to information you receive from your child's school, we strongly suggest you:

1) Get an independent assessment of your child's reading speed and comprehension. **Comprehension** is often the key issue, because reading comprehension will be more important than ever for math, science, and social studies. *Reading comprehension, at or above grade level, is the most critical skill necessary to pass the new much harder assessments.* Too often schools have told parents their child is reading close to grade level. The school reading results usually refer to reading fluency, which is how well your child reads out loud.

The key to measure reading comprehension is how well your child understands what he or she reads silently, which is often a year or two lower than reading fluency, even for a child entering 3rd grade.

2) Find out from your child's teacher what strategies he or she uses that work for your child. Not every method is equally effective for all students.

3) Get the right help from your child's school. At present, obtaining an evaluation can be difficult, and implementing the appropriate plans can be almost as difficult. If you contact us directly, we can offer additional information to help you be informed and empowered at accelerating the evaluation process, to put the right plans in place.

4) If your child is significantly behind or has the potential to do better, get your child the help your child needs. This is more obvious when your child is well below grade level, **but it is just as important when your smart or even gifted child is at or just below grade level**. We had a school tell parents, whose son was at the 55th percentile, that there was no need for the parents to do anything extra for their child.

Although these scores are above passing level, they were not indicative of what was possible to achieve for this child. The parent persisted. With our help, the parents' and the student's hard work, he was able to improve his test scores to the 98th percentile. This student later:

a.   Was in the top 10th percentile of his high school class

b.   Was very successful in advanced classes in middle and high school

c.   Was able to excel at a private school, where the psychologist and the headmaster had initially suggested the parents be more realistic and go elsewhere.

5) We encourage every parent to go the extra mile to collaborate with your child's teacher or teachers and the other staff at school. We have seen numerous cases where a teacher was supposed to sign an agenda to make sure the assignments were correctly written. While this was followed for a few days, it stopped. When the parents countersign that the work is completed and put in a place where the student knows where to find it, the teachers are far more cooperative.

Proactive Parents Make The Difference

Every year we get desperate calls in February, March, and even April to help children get ready for the upcoming 3rd Grade FCAT, or other tests. We are not miracle workers.

The time to start getting the right help for your child is NOW.

First, understand your child's:
- Present level of reading speed and comprehension
- Strengths and issues that are holding him or her back
- Potential to do far better

If you find your child has a reading comprehension challenge, learns differently, and has a combination of challenges, we recommend that you:

Isolate your child's needs.
If your child has a significant reading comprehension challenge, learns differently, and has a visual processing, attention, and/or anxiety challenge, you want to consider a program that integrates improving **the relevant issues,** while teaching the way your child learns best.

Commit to take action NOW

To start the process visit our website at
www.3dlearner.com/success-assessment
and complete the on-line **Success Assessment** with your child.

3D Learner
7100 W Camino Real, Suite 215
Boca Raton, FL 33433
Tel 561-361-7495
parents@3dlearner.com
www.3dlearner.com/3rd-grade

Follow us on:

www.3dlearner.com/blog

 www.facebook.com/3dlearner

 www.twitter.com/3dlearner

 www.linkedin.com/3dlearner

"You showed us our daughter's gifts and helped transform her into an outrageously successful student."
Dr. and Mrs. Robert Rehnke, St. Petersburg, FL

"We wanted to report that our daughter continues her success in school and third grade. She raised her FCAT scores from 3 in reading and math to 4 and 5…. Most importantly though, she is really enjoying her success and is much more confident. Thanks for everything"
M. Gill, Boca Raton, FL

"I want to thank you and your family at 3D Learner for being such a wonderful answer to prayer!
You and Mark are true advocates for children who are trying to find their voice."
M. Couch, Grandma from TN

"I remain forever grateful to you for teaching me to deal with dyslexia. Without your help I would never have been able to graduate from Stetson University nor even consider the possibility of law school. From the bottom of my heart…I thank you!"
K. Bass, Former student, Deland, FL

"Thank you all at 3D Learner for your time and dedication to this program. We are seeing much improvement, and the "home front" is becoming more stress-free each day (big smile)."
A Holmes, Ft. Lauderdale, FL

"My daughter is in 5th grade, and has been steadily improving in her reading each year since we came to see you in Florida, at the end of 1st grade. We diligently did our "Flearning" exercises for many months, and that was definitely the turning point, after months of trying the traditional phonics approach with very limited success. Just as important, you taught ME the invaluable lesson of different learning styles, and made me see the many strengths in my child that are often ignored or under-appreciated by our traditional schools. This knowledge has made parenting her much more pleasant, and has allowed me to steer her in directions that I know will yield success.

Mostly, I wanted to give hope to other parents out there that with time, maturity, and diligence, a right-brained "dyslexic" child with ADHD can become an engaged, enthusiastic student. For the third time this week my daughter has expressed how much she is enjoying her current mystery book (totally on grade-level!), and wants me to buy her more books by the same author. These are words I never thought I'd hear this child say! How many nights I lost sleep wondering if we'd ever even get this child through high school . . . Thank you for all you do, and for offering an out-of-the-box solution that really works!"

L. McHale, Montville, NJ